EXCERPTS FROM
THE HEART OF A MOM

the Heart of a Mom

A CONSCIOUS APPROACH TO PARENTING

ISBN 978-0-9856363-0-2

Published by LiveThroughTheHeart, LLC
P.O. Box 241759
Los Angeles, CA 90024
424-442-9562

www.livethroughtheheart.com.

Editor: Debbie Anderson

Cover Design: Ty Webb

Author Photo: Rebekah Jelsing

Printed and bound in the U.S.A. by ballbookfactory.com

"My intention as a parent is to be present and authentically parent my child in a way that supports, protects, and inspires him to live to his potential as a human being in this universe."

I dedicate this book to my son Jaden-Cole, who inspires me each and every day to live through my heart. My greatest gift in life has been the opportunity to be your mother. Thank you for your wisdom and quite simply, for being the beautiful boy that you are.

CONTENTS

EXCERPTS FROM THE HEART OF A MOM

ACKNOWLEDGEMENTS

I am filled with gratitude to be able to share this book with all of you. I want to thank my ex-husband David for urging me to share my ideas with the world by creating this book. I at many times questioned my abilities and am grateful for his support and his belief in me and in this project. Throughout the difficulty of our separation and divorce he has managed to offer his guidance and encouragement. I am grateful to all he has added to this project, my life, and our family.

I am forever grateful to my parents who have provided me with challenges that have allowed me to understand the world and consider alternate perspectives. Although our relationship has not always been an easy one, it is a relationship that has formulated the person that I am today. It is through my relationship with them that I have been able to come to parent in the way that I have chosen and written in this book. I thank them for their continued love and support.

I deeply appreciate the support and guidance from a very special friend, Aprille Chaffin. Throughout the many twists and turns my life has experienced over the last five years Aprille has offered me her wisdom and guidance. She has exemplified the strength and willingness to confront me with difficult truths when necessary. I am eternally grateful for all I have learned from her both about the world at large and about myself.

I am also indebted to all the beautiful mothers that I come into contact with and learn from daily. It is through all of you that I am inspired to challenge myself and truly strive to come to understand this beautiful gift of parenting at a deeper level. I learn from you, I honor you, and I respect you. I am blessed to be a mother and to share this very important job of parenting with you all.

Finally I want to thank all the beautiful children throughout the world. Their honesty, wisdom, and willingness to simply be are an inspiration to me each and every day.

INTRODUCTION: MY STORY

I am many things, and most importantly to me, a mom. I live in Southern California with my beautiful son and am fortunate to work as a stay-at-home mother. I realize that I am in no way an expert, and so am simply sharing my experiences in an area where I believe most of us struggle -- parenting. In my personal journey as a parent, I have undergone a tremendous amount of growth. As a result, I feel that motherhood is the most amazing experience this universe has to offer me.

I began writing this book when my son was approximately 18 months old. I spent the next few years gathering information to create what I have written here, which is the unique way I view my son and how I choose to raise him. This is very different from how my parents raised me, and how I see many parents around me raise their children. I do not think my way is better or worse, it just works for me, and so I have chosen to share it with other parents. Perhaps you are looking for some inspiration in your own parenting journey, or would like to add some of what is included in this book to what you already do. As for me, I've raised my son as a married woman, with and without help from a nanny, and as a single mom. It is my sincere wish that some of the philosophies I have written here might fit into your life whatever your family looks like, and makes all our parenting challenges just a little bit easier.

I wrote this book in short excerpts as the words poured from my heart onto the page because I wanted to keep it simple. I believe that we can parent with simplicity if we stop and breathe, remain present, and stay open. I have watched others struggle with so many issues when it came to their children and thought that maybe my parenting style might help eliminate some of the frustration so many parents face. As a mother, I learn something new every day, and as I have grown, I have written.

WHO I AM

I grew up in Blauvelt, which is a small town about 30 minutes north of New York City. I considered myself an only child even though I was the youngest of five siblings. I was born twelve years after my closest-aged sibling, while my oldest sister and I have twenty years between us. For this reason, my parents were much older than my friends' parents were at the time. My parents and I had more than a generation separating us and I think that contributed to our difficulty in relating to one another.

Throughout my childhood, I felt as though nobody really understood me. I was a sensitive and empathetic individual. From a young age, I can remember fighting with my parents over things like people's skin color and then running to my room crying, not understanding their beliefs. Their close-minded attitudes left me feeling angry and alone and completely misunderstood. I can remember them laughing at my perspective and telling me I didn't know what I was talking about when we fought. From that memory, I clearly remember the pain I felt in my heart, and the confusion regarding where I fit in the world.

So there I was, an alien in my own home trying to find a way to feel confident about the person I was becoming, and the feelings in my heart about the world around me. I didn't like being home and found ways to escape. I would head to friends' homes as often as I could. When I was home, I would read books constantly to withdraw to fantasy worlds where I could lose myself. I would stay in my room and listen to music or talk on the phone. I tried to have as little contact as I could with the people who lived in my house.

Let me interject to write that I don't blame my parents or believe they were bad people. They were from a different generation and doing the best they could with what they knew. They worked hard to make sure I was well cared for, sent me to private schools, attended most events in which I participated, and above all, loved me. They did not intend to cause me pain or sadness. I was simply different from all that they knew and they had a hard time recognizing, accepting, and supporting that difference.

That said, I also grew up in a home where there was constant fighting. My parents would scream and yell at one another and at me so loudly that our neighbors could hear them. I remember sitting on my bed with my hands over my ears and the covers over my head sobbing and wishing they would just stop. I would pray that they would get a divorce so I didn't have to hear the fighting anymore. They would even fight in public places such as restaurants and I can remember making deals with them so they would stop, including promises like, "I'll clean my room and do the dishes at home if you stop fighting now." Looking back, I don't remember that working even once.

My feeling misunderstood, coupled with the constant warring in my home, made for a difficult childhood. As a young girl, I was a perfectionist, and the "good daughter" who did everything right. I never got into trouble, was at the top of my class, had friends, always kept my room clean, participated in sports and extracurricular activities, and looked "pretty." I was constantly trying to please everyone around me to make peace.

Then somewhere around the age of eight, I became angry. I was no longer able to ignore my parent's beliefs as their unfair and unjustified rules began to interfere with my life and relationships. For example, my mother would not allow me to be friends with a schoolmate because her mother was not a stay-at-home mom. I began rebelling against my parents and speaking my mind, with most of the conflict occurring between my mother and me. My father was not home very often and so he managed to remain disengaged from most of the turmoil.

Upon entering high school, my life of rebellion truly began. During my freshman year, I began to date someone who was no longer in high school and took classes at the community college. He drove, smoked cigarettes, drank alcohol, did drugs, and eventually became both emotionally and physically abusive. At the age of fourteen, I lost my virginity after only one month of dating him. I found myself completely dependent and before I knew it, my entire world revolved around him. I no longer had any friends of my own. I completely withdrew from all sports and activities. My life was about my boyfriend and I was terrified of losing him.

After dating for one year, the physical abuse began. I will never forget the first time it happened. We were arguing and I was crying because he was mad at me and I was so scared I would lose him. Out of nowhere, he hit me across the face. I was shocked. I continued to cry and plead with him to stop being so angry. He calmed down and we began to talk. In the middle of our conversation, he became angry again and kicked me in the face. I was sobbing and he was laughing. Then somehow, we were having sex and all I could think was how much I loved him and how grateful I was that he didn't leave me. The next two years were filled with violence and humiliation that I couldn't share with anyone.

Somehow, through all of this, a little voice inside my heart seemed to be guiding me to some greater good. I kept good grades in spite of cutting class, sneaking out of my house at night, drinking, and smoking pot. At the age of 16, I put myself into therapy without telling my parents. I found a way to pay for it on a sliding scale and would sneak to my individual and group therapy sessions. I knew this was not something my parents would approve of or allow me to continue. I did this for over a year and eventually decided to go away to college. My boyfriend and I broke up about two months into my freshman year.

I made friends and enjoyed the freedom college offered. It was during this time that my son's father and I began dating. We had been friends for over a year and suddenly found ourselves very much in love. We stayed together for the next sixteen years.

My relationship with my husband was rooted very deeply in our love for one another. We were kids when we began dating and I believe that was why we needed each other more than is healthy. We became codependent and didn't see ourselves as separate individuals. I can look back now and see that I lost myself in him and put his needs above my own.

Over time, I began feeling underappreciated and resentful. We tried very hard to make our relationship work and found ourselves in therapy, reading self-help books, and trying creative ways to keep our relationship alive. These things would help somewhat, but we never seemed to be able to find true happiness with one another. It seemed that when my husband and I were good, we were great, and when we were bad, we were really bad. As we became respectively more independent, we found ourselves growing apart. It turned out that we had very different life goals and priorities and it seemed time to move on from our relationship.

The process of divorce is like death. There were moments when I didn't know how I would make it through and couldn't imagine things getting better. I cried so much that I looked forward to the tears because after a good cry, I released pain and revealed a new layer of myself. During the divorce, I promised myself one year of staying single and refraining from dating. I spent the year diving deeply into me. I wanted to feel every inch of the pain, and understand and learn from it. I wanted to stand on my own two feet and overcome this obstacle without any sort of crutch. I am proud of this and of where I am today.

WHY I WROTE THIS BOOK

As you read this, you might wonder why I am including it in a book about parenting. I didn't come from a perfect family. Rather, I struggled with and overcame many obstacles. Still, I found a way to listen to my inner voice and continue forward. I managed to find a more effective way to live in the world and ultimately, to parent differently than I was parented. This book is my effort to share what I learned, often the hard way.

After college I decided to go to graduate school and received a Masters in Clinical Social Work. Throughout my life I have always had a desire to help others and can remember having the dream of making a difference in the world. For these reasons I made the decision to become a social worker. For a time I was a rape crisis counselor, I worked at a children's hospital with dying and disabled children and their families, I provided therapy to children and families at a counseling center, I counseled individuals addicted to drugs and alcohol, and I was an Emergency Room/Hospital Social Worker. Many of the situations that I bore witness to are heartbreaking and disturbing. There were times I had to take babies away from their parents, hold abused children in my arms, listen to parents crying through their struggle to connect with their children, and listen to children full of anger and feeling completely invisible. My days were filled with guiding others out of crisis and toward more healthy ways of existing. These experiences have had a lasting effect on me and contribute to my writing this book. I have witnessed first hand the importance of consciously parenting in a way that honors and respects our children at the core.

On a personal note, I also have to admit that at one time, I believed I had proof that having children just wasn't worth it. I watched as mothers around me made their lives about their children and soon enough, they didn't know themselves anymore. I heard a laundry list of complaints about having no free time, feeling completely exhausted all day every day, and experiencing constant frustration.

These tales of woe were not only limited to motherhood,

but also about the difficulties associated with having children. I heard about tantrums, sleepless nights, arguments, anger and frustration. From the outside looking in, I just couldn't see the point in going down the path of parenthood.

Fast forward a few years and my close friends began having babies. During their pregnancies, I began to connect to the other, more beautiful aspects of parenting. Suddenly, that biological clock women speak so much about started ticking. As time went by, the ticking grew louder and louder and louder. I had officially changed my mind and now, more than anything, I wanted to have a baby. I was so excited when I became pregnant, and convinced I would find a way to make my experience as a mother extraordinary.

WHAT I BELIEVE

My job as a mother is to love and protect my child in an openhearted way, to foster his innate wisdom and help him remain connected to his authentic self. This style of parenting focuses on changing two major perceptions. First, we need to be open to transforming how we view our children. Second, we need to alter our perception of our role as parents. Through it all, we need to remain constantly present in the moment.

I like to believe that we all love our children and want the best for them. Sometimes our habits and learned behaviors are so ingrained that we fall back into them without even thinking. We simply don't realize we can parent differently.

As far as how we view our children, it's no secret that throughout history, children have been treated as less than adults. We've all heard expressions such as, "Children should be seen and not heard," "Children should only speak when spoken to," or comments such as, "Oh, you're just a child," or "You'll understand when you grow up." Parents can also tend to view their children as possessions. There can be attempts to mold children into what parents want them to be or what they think they should be in the future. Children somehow take on the responsibility for how their parent wants to be seen by the outside world. We become so concerned with what others will think or say about us regarding something our child does or the way he/she behaves.

From the time of conception, our children are wise. They have the ability to connect, understand, and communicate. They have the ability to reconnect us to the wisdom we hold inside of us. They have the ability to transform the world if we will only open our hearts and minds and listen.

When it comes to our role as parents, it is essential to guide our children in a way that honors them and keeps them connected to their authentic selves. Many of us have experienced feeling lost and have sought to find ourselves, whether we realize it or not.

Some of us realize we have lost sight of who we really are and some of us are unsure. Look at the self-help industry. There are books, groups, and workshops all geared to help us find our way. When we feel misunderstood or unseen by others, conflict occurs. I wonder how much of this "feeling lost" could be avoided had our authenticity been fostered from the beginning. If we see our children as they really are, then maybe we can eliminate a great deal of the conflict within us and our children. Parenting from the the heart means seeing our children for who they are and being open to their wisdom and all we can learn from them. It involves a willingness to allow our children to be their own people. Above all, it means loving them for who they are in the deepest part of themselves.

In the following excerpts, I share more of my personal experiences and beliefs to illustrate how I strive to remain openhearted with my son.

EXCERPTS FROM

the Heart *of a* Mom

penned by Jennifer Laurent

THINK POSITIVE AND GET EDUCATED

It all comes down to how you think and
what you know.

Once I decided I wanted to have a baby, I began envisioning the way things were going to go. The way some little girls imagine one day being a bride, I began to put together a mental picture of what lie ahead. This is where my relationship with my child began. At the time, I had no idea what was in store, but I clearly remember being conscious of how I wanted to parent.

What is most important is that my picture of the future was a positive one. My mental imagery included visions of a child who slept well, a relationship with my child based on respect and trust, and mutual understanding. I didn't envision things being perfect and easy, but I did look forward to parenthood with the knowledge that my positive intentions would give me the strength to parent in a different way than I experienced as a child. I truly believed that parenting would be whatever I chose to make it, and that I could create the parenting experience that I envisioned. It was this sense of faith that lent power to my intentions to parent with an open and positive heart.

I began to read in an effort to understand the different ideas and schools of thought on parenting. I sifted through many books and took from each the concepts that felt right for my family and me. I was educating myself, and through that education, my confidence to parent grew. Even before my child was born, I felt ready. It's funny that we spend so much time in school learning a trade or profession, but no time educating ourselves to be parents. Most of us never even think about it until it happens and then we find ourselves unprepared and stressed, which can create fear and anxiety. Fear and anxiety can often make it more difficult to think clearly. Decisions made in this manner tend to be clouded rather than based in clarity. It becomes difficult then to feel secure in the decisions we do make.

The reality of it is that so much of parenting involves unpredictability and unpreparedness, that if we can develop our own foundation, beliefs, and intentions regarding parenting before becoming a parent, we will be able to apply those concepts to the crazy situations we will undoubtedly face daily. Even after becoming a parent, reframing our intentions and mindsets can change the way we discipline and teach our children. We can open our hearts and minds at any time, we just need to decide to do it. Knowledge, preparedness, and openness create confidence and the ability to relax in situations that might otherwise cause frustration.

Often times we say that parents are "lucky" when they have what looks to be an easy child. I don't believe in luck. As Roman philosopher Seneca reportedly said, "Luck is what happens when preparation meets opportunity." I don't think that an "easy" child comes from luck, but rather from preparation. Pregnancy represents a beautiful opportunity to prepare ourselves as parents. During this time, we can set our intention for the upcoming parent-child experience. We can then begin gathering the knowledge and skills necessary to make that intention happen in the way we envision.

If your child is older and you want to apply this concept,

you can take a step back and observe him or her. Think about what you have learned about your child to this point. Also, take note of yourself. Take an honest inventory of your feelings, motivations, struggles, and joys. Be willing to find new ways for what you're doing that might not be working. Read, take a class, ask other parents. It's never too late to improve any situation or to prepare.

BE OPEN TO THE LESSONS

There is a lesson in everything.
Your job is to find it and apply it.

Life might not always go the way you think, but you quickly learn that the universe knows better. For me, finding out I was having a boy was definitely unexpected. When I imagined having a child, I pictured a beautiful little girl, with dresses and dolls, and pictured having mother-daughter discussions about boys, safety, and sex. In truth, the thought of parenting a boy scared me. I wasn't sure I would know how to raise a little boy and what I thought would be the extra mess, aggression, and noise.

Then I got pregnant and knew immediately I was having a boy. You know that intuition us mothers seem to get? Still, after my 20-week ultrasound, I had the doctor hide the results in an envelope and went to a restaurant with my husband to read it together. We opened the envelope and saw "It's A Boy!" written inside. Tears came to my eyes and I thought, "I have no clue how to raise a boy!"

Fast forward to the present and now I realize I was meant to parent a son. Through him, I have learned about myself and expanded my ability to love. I have reconnected with parts of my heart and soul that I had completely forgotten. For example, as my son grew, I remembered very clearly that I was a tomboy as a child in New York. I can't tell you how wonderful it feels to have reconnected with that part of my identity and allow it to thrive.

I also believe that parenting my son has allowed some of my unresolved issues and insecurities to present themselves and given me the opportunity to work through and heal them. I have often wondered if these unresolved areas would have interfered with my ability to parent a daughter. I honestly will never know, but I am certain that my son has helped me grow beyond description.

We might not always understand why something happens in our lives, and we may wonder at the absolute unfairness of it all, but there truly is always a reason and a lesson. The key is to find both and learn from them. I know it can be hard. Believe me, I've had the opportunity to learn quite a few difficult lessons in my life. The first step is to make a conscious choice to be receptive and open ourselves to the idea that there is something to learn from our challenges. This openness makes space for the lesson to appear. After gaining what we can from it, we are free to move forward.

IT'S ALL ABOUT ENERGY

Keep the energy moving and you can move
through challenges that arise.
Stay stagnant and the energy stays
stagnant within you.

I was thrilled to be pregnant, but physically, I felt like I had the flu every day for months. I was nauseated, tired, and starving, yet had no appetite. The last thing I wanted to do was exercise. I had the very strong desire to sit on the couch watching television, and not move an inch. Nevertheless, I was on a mission to get through my pregnancy working out, looking good, and feeling great. I was determined to be a thriving pregnant woman.

Every single day I forced myself, sometimes kicking and screaming, to the gym or a yoga class. I noticed after exercising, I felt a little better. Once I made this connection, I started to pay attention to how I felt and when. What I realized was that if I didn't feel well and just stayed in bed, then I would continue to feel awful throughout the day. If I got up and went to the gym, yoga, or walking trail, I felt good.

It hit me that everything is energy. If we are not feeling well, then it makes sense to move that "bad" energy out to make way for new and healthier energy. If we stay stagnant, then that unhealthy energy has difficulty moving out of our bodies. Exercise kept my energy circulating, and so I managed to stay active up until the day I delivered.

I also realized that this idea of everything being energy extended beyond the physical. Our emotions, thoughts, and beliefs are also energy forms and can be moved out of our bodies and transformed. Perhaps we are angry, impatient, or anxious. We need to first honor the way we feel. We need to acknowledge and accept what is happening and furthermore, not judge ourselves for it. Simple statements like "Of course I am feeling this way" or "It's ok that I am feeling this way" can validate a sense of non-judgment. Once we are able to breathe love and acceptance into any discomfort inside ourselves, we then allow room for that discomfort to shift into something else.

As much as we love our children, they can have the ability to push our buttons and trigger frustration, annoyance and even anger. As you know, it's important that we don't hold onto these feelings and let them persist within us. By acknowledging how we feel to ourselves and sometimes even to our child – "Mommy is feeling very frustrated right now and needs to regroup" -- we can begin to move those feelings or negative energy out of our system.

This has the added benefit of teaching our children that when they are sitting in frustration or anger, they can learn ways to move it out of their bodies. Maybe they need to wiggle or dance or yell. Perhaps a good laugh will help. No matter the method, we can move negative energy out of the way and transform it into something positive.

EMBRACE THE POWER OF THE MIND-BODY CONNECTION

Be present in the moment, even when
it's uncomfortable.

When I was eight weeks pregnant, I took a prenatal yoga class. Up until then, I had been doing Ashtanga, which is a very vigorous form of yoga. When I became pregnant, I couldn't keep up with the practice, so I went to a gentler class. At first, this was a very difficult transition for me. I remember feeling frustrated with the new instruction because it moved so much slower. I was bored and irritated, and had to force myself to continue to attend.

After a few weeks, I settled down and allowed myself to relax. All at once, I was consciously breathing and slowly but surely, feeling in touch with every inch of my body, inside and out. I felt myself connecting with the tiniest parts of me all the way down to my toes. As the months went on,

I became more and more connected and centered. I felt in control of my body and mind.

The class allowed me to experience an alternate way of being, which connected me to my unborn child at a very deep level. I was no longer rushing around and distracting myself. I was just breathing and letting my inner wisdom guide me. It was during this process I gained valuable insight that would help with my upcoming role as a mother.

One very important lesson I learned during this yoga class was that I had a hard time simply sitting. I was used to a life where I constantly challenged and pushed myself. When I began taking this class, I realized that I needed to be still, breathe and stay in the moment. Sometimes this forced inaction seemed boring, other times I became agitated. I can even remember feeling physically ill some moments. Eventually though, I learned to sit in a way that calmed my mind and gave me insight.

I had no idea how important this lesson would be for me as a mother. After I brought my son home from the hospital, I needed to be still to feed him, quiet him, and lull him to sleep. I found myself able to meet his needs and be there with him in a calm and patient way. I didn't feel the rush or agitation that I know I would have felt had I not learned in my yoga class that I had impatient tendencies, and needed to embrace stillness.

I also realized how important it is to be present in the moment. By breathing and focusing my mind, I could center and ground myself. I am sure so many of us moms know how fragmented we can feel at times. I sometimes feel like I am split in so many different directions that I have a hard time getting a handle on any single one. When this happens, my chest tightens and I have trouble taking full and deep breaths. Learning to breathe and center myself has been a vital tool I apply to parenting to bring the situation back into focus.

THIS JOURNEY IS OUR CHILD'S, NOT OURS

From the moment of conception, the child's life journey begins.

I had always heard women speak about labor and delivery with such horror. I am sure you have too. I remember the stories recounting the awful pain, long labors, c-sections, and on and on. These stories can be downright terrifying, and next thing you know, you are imagining the worst.

As I prepared for the day I was to give birth to my son, I realized I was excited and not feeling fear and anxiety. I had learned to avoid the birthing horror stories by kindly asking women to share their negative experiences with me only after I had delivered my son. I committed to thinking of the delivery process as a positive experience and envisioned exactly how beautiful it would be when the day arrived.

I decided to practice a birthing method called hypno-birthing. This involved a daily practice of breathing exercises, relaxation, and visualization techniques to stay focused and centered throughout labor and delivery. Using this technique, I stayed tuned to the reality that birth is a natural process that does not have to be painful. I believed that if I removed my fears, anxiety, and tension, and allowed my body to relax, I would have an enjoyable birth process.

As I continued to prepare and get closer to the day I would finally meet my son, I began to embrace the act of birthing. I realized that it was important to think about the way I wanted it to be, and then to let it go. I knew that ultimately I was not in full control. I needed to be open to whatever possibilities presented themselves.

I began to see my son as my teammate in the birthing process. He and I would be working together. I began speaking to him about it and letting him know that I would be respectful of his entry into the world. I realized that this was his journey and he would be utilizing me, literally my body, to enter life outside the womb. In a sense, as his mother, I was simply the medium. So I let it go. I allowed my son to decide when he would enter the world and kept reassuring him that we were partners, helping one other through the process of birth. I promised I would listen to him every step of the way.

This concept of letting go and ultimately acceptance allows us to be fully open. The process can then unfold without our perceptions and fears altering or hindering that process in any way. There was a freedom in surrendering. Not only for me, but I imagine for my son as well.

Now that he's in this world I continue to let go. I believe that my child is not "mine." My child is his own person. I have simply been gifted with giving him life and being his parent during this part of his journey. I am here to support him and keep him safe so that he can live to his potential, whatever that may be for him. He is separate from me and I strive every day to make him as independent, strong, and knowledgeable as I can. I want to provide him with every tool possible so he can make this journey as full, far, and wide as possible. I want him to see that there are no limitations to what he can achieve in this life and to what this life can provide him. I have no preconceived notions or expectations as to what he may become in the future. My only hope for him is that whatever he does, he does it passionately from his heart. Whether I agree with his decisions or not, my job is to love him and accept this is his life and journey, which is separate from mine.

SET YOUR INTENTION FOR THE MOTHER YOU CHOOSE TO BE

Decide your purpose as a parent, and live it every day.

I have observed many decisions made from fear or because we believe we "should" do things in certain ways. We don't necessarily understand why we are deciding the way we do, and yet we proceed anyway. We then end up doubting ourselves in the face of disagreement and judgment. I have not only witnessed this happen, I've been guilty of it myself. In the end, the discontent that results is inescapable. I knew I did not want to make parenting decisions without a foundation that allowed me to understand my motivations, and certainly did not want to feel the awful second-guessing that resulted when I decided for the wrong reasons.

So in preparing myself to be a mother, I considered what kind of parent I wanted to be, which included my approach to discipline, boundaries I would set, and goals for what type of family I wanted. I then chose my intention: to be present and authentically parent my child in a way that supports, protects, and inspires him to fulfill his potential as a human being in this universe. I want decisions about my child and family to come from a place inside my heart that feels right. I want there to be a purpose for the things I do and the choices I make. There will always be people around me who disagree and give sound reasons as to why I am wrong, but with my intention set, I have a clear understanding of my reasoning, and confidence in the choices I make.

The more clearly you are able to state your intention, the more direction and confidence you will have as you move through the daily act of parenting. An intention needs to be a personal decision that feels good. I suggest you honestly take into account who you are as a human being, your morals and values, beliefs, expectations, , and limitations. Once your intention is set, refer to it often and allow it to guide you as you parent. It is never too late to set this intention and can be done at any point during your parenting journey.

As I mentioned, setting intentions makes us more secure

in our roles as parents. Having confidence in ourselves allows our children to have confidence in us. This frees us from uncertainty, and clearly sets the direction we want things to go, with a general guideline for how we want our family to be and grow. This freedom allows simplicity to exist in day-to-day family life, which can bring forth the fun and lightheartedness that makes parenting such a joyous experience.

WE DO NOT NEED WORDS TO COMMUNICATE

We rely on verbal communication far too much and
forget that there are other more effective
ways to understand one another.

When newborn babies come into this world they expect to be understood. They are born with the ability to communicate, just not verbally. In addition, they expect that when they enter this world, their mothers will understand them and know exactly what they need.

Many times, this doesn't happen. Many of us do not understand our children. Not out of lack of love or trying, but simply because we do not realize there are other ways to understand. It's all too easy to believe that because children aren't speaking yet, they can't communicate. As a result, we make decisions for our children based on assumptions of what we believe is best for them. Sometimes, this is the total opposite of what the child is asking for or needs.

This initial miscommunication can have a lasting impact on the mother-child relationship. It can become the very first time a child is let down by his parent. As a mom continues to believe that her child doesn't know anything, and that she needs to make all decisions, absent of his input, the child begins to learn that he can't trust his parent to tune into his needs. The child's sense of being understood breaks down further and further until the child eventually feels misunderstood all the time.

Put another way, I've witnessed parents treat their children as blank slates, perhaps believing their children can't understand them since they aren't verbally communicating or not communicating well. I've also seen parents have inappropriate conversations in front of their children, based on the assumption that the children don't understand what they're saying. Furthermore, I've observed parents make decisions for their kids without including them in the process. Now fast forward to the teenage years when so many adolescents feel misunderstood. Teenagers constantly complain that their parents don't "get it," don't really see them, don't ever listen. They feel they can't go to their parents with concerns, problems, and questions. These kids are speaking the truth. And it isn't that parents are not trying. Parents are trying very hard to make sense of it all. Rather, this dynamic is a pattern that may have begun years ago, perhaps upon the newborn's arrival, when parents couldn't initially tune into their child's needs.

So, here is where we need to stop and really look into the eyes of our children. Look deeply and understand who they are on a soul level. Listen and communicate through connection, energy, senses, and feelings. Watch body language, facial expressions, and alertness. Truly seek to make a connection with your child that touches both of your souls. When something is not working, try something new until you begin to understand what your child is attempting to communicate.

When I say look into our children's eyes, I mean look with your heart fully open and willing to see beyond what you think you know. Do this and I believe you'll come to understand your child on a deeper level.

We can learn so much from our children simply by tapping into their profound wisdom. If you can connect with your child, you gain wisdom and clarity about yourself and him that you may never have thought possible. Imagine being able to get in touch with the insight and intuition you too had as a child and have somehow lost over time. Our children's connection to source, or whatever higher power you believe in, has the power to reconnect us with our higher self.

OUR BABIES DON'T NEED US NEARLY AS MUCH AS WE THINK THEY DO

"The worst thing that you can do for others is the things that they can do for themselves."

(Abraham Lincoln, paraphrased.)

I don't think our babies need us quite as much as we want to believe they do. Don't get me wrong, I realize newborns are physically helpless. They absolutely need us to survive. What I mean is that our babies don't need us to do every little thing for them and to step in as quickly as many of us do. They really are capable of becoming increasingly self-reliant as they grow.

For example, I found that if I gave my newborn son a chance to cry for small amounts of time without coming to his aid immediately, it gave him the ability to learn what was wrong and figure out ways to self soothe. By allowing him to cry it out in stages, I did not interfere with his process and rob him of the chance to figure things out for himself. Had I responded immediately he would not have learned ways to meet his own needs. It is so important for children to understand that they can rely on themselves as well as their mothers. The earlier children learn their own capabilities, the easier it will be for them to integrate these skills into and throughout their lives.

By jumping in to help right away, we end up making our children more dependent on us because they quickly learn that they don't know how to do things themselves. We want our kids to be self-sufficient and independent adults. It is through struggles and failures that we all learn. In providing our children with opportunities to struggle and fail, we are giving them the opportunity to grow.

Furthermore, it is important to ask ourselves why we are jumping in to help our children. If we have a clear understanding of our intentions and expectations before reacting, our compulsion to help so quickly might lessen. One reason we tend to help right away is to minimize our own discomfort. It isn't easy to watch someone struggle to work things out on his or her own. When this person is your growing child who is without the ability to communicate with words, not responding immediately becomes even more difficult and uncomfortable. However, as parents it is our job to find ease in our discomfort without passing it on to our children. If you really think about it, continuously coming to the rescue only works in the short term, but does both mother and child a disservice in the long run.

Another reason we rush to help is to fulfill our own needs. I think we should ask ourselves if we are using our children to meet certain needs or fill gaps in our lives. For example, do we use our children to feel loved and needed, to relieve our anger and frustration, or to be our friend? We need to get to a place where we can honestly say the opportunity to be their parent is all we need from our children. This allows children the freedom to move throughout their own life journey without guilt. If we rely on our children to fill our emotional needs, they become responsible for taking care of us. This is not their responsibility. It is our job as parents to care for our children, not the other way around.

One last reason we may rush to help too quickly is the overwhelming desire we all have to feel important. Everyone wants to feel that he or she is valued. I know I do. Do we want our children to depend on us? Does their dependence on us somehow make us feel more significant? It seems that many of us find our child's independence almost threatening to our sense of self worth. Sometimes our ability to fix everything for our children makes us feel as though we are necessary and irreplaceable in their lives. The thing is, we don't need to do every little thing for our children to achieve this importance. The role of being a parent, in and of itself, is as important as it gets.

When we find that we need additional validation of our importance, it helps to find what we feel passionate about in life and pursue those things. Through this, we will feel more fulfilled, our children will be inspired as they witness our own journey, and will also feel relieved as our sense of worth is no longer their responsibility.

I work every day to make my son a little more independent and self-reliant. I want him to know he can make it in this world on his own. I truly believe that his connections to others should come from love and reciprocity, rather than necessity.

I DON'T KNOW AND THAT'S OK!

"I don't know" is probably the most honest and liberating thing you can say, yet one of the hardest.

When I was young, my parents seemed to have all the answers. I believed everything they told me and trusted what they said. As I grew older, I discovered there were times when my parents were wrong. I began to see they told me certain things they knew to be untrue, such as "We can't go to the toy store because it is closed," rather than explain that it wasn't a good time for them to go and so on. I didn't realize it at the time, but looking back, I think when you find out your parents have told you intentional untruths, your trust in them starts to diminish.

I have noticed in myself, and in others, a very strong desire to seem like we know what we are doing at all times. Even with the little things, for some reason there is something wrong with not knowing. It's as if saying "I don't know" is something to be ashamed of and avoid. In motherhood, the pressure to have every answer to every question seems to increase tenfold. We seem to somehow internalize that if we don't know the answers, we are not good mothers. We think that people or our children may think less of us, judge, and criticize.

Another reason we try to have all the answers for our children is to make them feel safe. As we all know, uncertainty can feel scary and unsettling. We aim to avoid having our children feel this way, too. Instead, we can teach our children that uncertainty is okay and does not have to be scary. We can show them that they are safe even in the midst of not knowing. We can allow our children their feelings so they can navigate through uncertain moments throughout their lives with the sense that they don't have to figure everything out at once. What a beautiful skill for them to acquire; to be able to sit in a moment of complete uncertainty in peace and confidence, rather than anxiety and panic.

The willingness to accept and admit that we do not know everything make us better parents and teaches our children a valuable lesson. Being able to say, "I don't know," allows you to state your truth, negate the pressure, and buy time to find an answer that feels right in your heart.

All of this gives our children the chance to see us as real human beings, which is a very important reality check for kids, who might tend to view their parents as superhuman. It is important that we begin to show our children that we are not perfect. Whenever we aren't sure, "I don't know" is the most honest answer we can give. Our kids may consider us making up an answer or stating a guess as a truth to be a lie. Children will respect us more for being honest about the things we don't know than pretending to know the things we don't. Finally, we give our children the opportunity to find the answers themselves.

I'M SORRY!

Simple apologies tell your children you respect
them and that you aren't perfect.

Throughout my life, my mother told me she was my parent and so didn't have to apologize to me. I'm not exactly sure why, but my mom felt pretty strongly that children did not deserve apologies. I can tell you that this hurt me, and I felt as though my feelings were often not validated. This divided my mom and I, leaving me feeling a lack of connection with her.

Sometimes in our attempt to seem like we know what we are doing at all times, we forget that we are human beings and make mistakes. We especially want our children to believe that we know what we are doing. Many parents don't want to be questioned or "undermined" in any way. My understanding is that when children question their parents, parents can sometimes feel this threatens their position or authority.

It seems to me that we place this impossible standard on ourselves to somehow be perfect and do everything correctly. It then becomes an embarrassment to make a mistake when we are parents. Yet, it's normal to make mistakes. We wash our colors with whites, we argue when we shouldn't, we hurt a friend's feelings. We make mistakes daily, and hopefully we are able to apologize when necessary. So then wouldn't it make sense that we would make mistakes in parenting, the hardest job in the world? Furthermore, doesn't it follow that our children deserve apologies when our mistakes hurt them?

By telling ourselves it's normal to mess up, acknowledging what we have done, and then apologizing, our children can learn so many valuable lessons. We can teach them it is OK to make mistakes and be wrong. They don't need to be perfect. This alone would allow them the freedom to take risks and venture out of their comfort zones without the fear of being reprimanded or feeling ashamed if they don't succeed. The fact of the matter is we need to be willing to fail in order to take the necessary risks for success in our lives. We can teach our children to find ease in saying I did my best, and I'm sorry I fell short of the mark for whatever reason.

We can also teach our children to stay connected to the fact that their actions and words can affect others. Often we are caught up in the "why." We need to remember that we all have reasons we do the things we do and say the things we say. Most often, they seem like very good reasons at the time. Reasons don't necessarily make things right and they certainly don't take away someone else's pain or sadness. In the end, no matter how great those reasons were, if we hurt someone, then we need to apologize. Even if only because saying sorry is the kind thing to do.

When we don't apologize to our children for the mistakes we make with them, they can become hurt and sad, and we can become disconnected from them as human beings. Yes, we are responsible for keeping our children safe and protected and therefore need to maintain some authority, but we can and should remain connected to them at a human and/or soul level, and treat them as we would any other person, regardless of age.

I make sure to apologize to my son whenever I make mistakes. Even when he was a baby, I made sure that I acknowledged the things I did wrong. By apologizing for the small things, children learn that their feelings and perceptions are valid. It also becomes easier to apologize for the larger things when you've practiced with the smaller ones. I can tell you that sometimes apologizing is not easy. There are moments when the last thing I want to do is be vulnerable and say I am sorry, but I know I must. I know that it is essential to the relationship I am building with my son.

For example, I may lose my temper or patience and take it out on him. Or I make a promise and forget to follow through with it. Other times, I may simply tune out and forget to pay attention to him and his needs. All of these things deserve acknowledgement and apology. Our children are noticing our mistakes, especially the ones that hurt their feelings or invalidate them as human beings. We all do this, it is impossible not to, I know. Making mistakes does not make us bad parents. The key is to be willing to admit it and own it. Our children may be noticing, but they are not judging. They love us and hearing us apologize to them can be a simple affirmation of just how much we love them. By doing this, we let our children know we are listening and paying attention, that we are monitoring our own actions and willing to admit that we are not perfect, and that we make mistakes and are open to try again. These lessons are invaluable to a child's growth into a loving human being.

FOCUS...FOCUS...FOCUS

It is only when you tune in that you see the reality of what is in front of you

Parenting takes focus. As we all know, this is not an easy task and at times, can seem close to impossible. We lose focus for so many reasons. We go on autopilot and next thing you know, we find ourselves driving to work when we should be driving to the grocery store. We go through the motions. We become distracted and end up half in our present situation and half in the argument we had the night before or the issues we are having at work.

This same lack of focus can show up in our relationships. We tend to make assumptions and set expectations based on past experiences, and forget to stay in the present moment. It then makes sense that we rely on these assumptions and expectations as crutches to get through moments when we are not fully present. We make statements like "that is just the way my child is" or we might make "never" and/or "always" statements about him. When we begin to group and label our children's behavior, we forget to look at what is really happening. Most of this occurs without our even realizing it.

It is during the times when I am unfocused and making assumptions that I find my child acting out and trying to make me listen. Through negative behaviors he is simply saying "Mom, listen to me!" When I am able to snap out of distraction, and realize what I have been doing, I quickly see that I have not been listening and tuning into the moment. I see that I was using assumptions patterned in my brain to move through the situation, not really sure of why. I can then acknowledge to my son that I was distracted, apologize, and really focus on what he is saying and needing in the moment. Once this happens, the acting out is no longer necessary and we can move forward. For us, moving forward involves a big hug along with some deep cleansing breaths, some laughter, and a lot of love.

As an example, my son loves to procrastinate at bedtime. Not only does he love to put off going to bed, he's mastered the art. When he was about two-and-a-half, I was trying to get him to sleep and he kept telling me that he couldn't sleep because his bed wasn't in the right spot. He insisted that his bed should be on the other side of the room. After a long and exhausting day, I automatically assumed he was again trying to avoid bedtime. I eventually left the room flabbergasted, and told him to go to sleep. He persisted and somehow got me back into his bedroom. I noticed that the air conditioner was on and my son was able to show me that he wanted to move the bed because the air blew on him when he slept and made him cold. My assumptions and expectations obscured my seeing the present situation for what it was right then. I immediately acknowledged what he was telling me, apologized for not listening better, and then proceeded to move the bed so he could sleep comfortably.

We all find ourselves losing focus briefly throughout the day, but there are also times when we go through rough patches in our lives. At these times, we may be distracted for days or even weeks. Our child's behavior can be a clue as to how we are handling our tough times. If we notice ongoing poor behavior, acting out, or disconnection in our relationship, it can be a sign that we aren't being present and are perhaps distracted with our own lives. The great thing about this is that the more we practice regaining focus with our children during the little daily losses of focus, the more adept we will become at remaining focused during more challenging times.

HONESTY IS THE BEST POLICY

We should only speak words that are true,
necessary, and kind.

(Sri Sathya Sai Baba, paraphrased)

Living an honest life is important to me, and I hope to inspire the same in my son. Honesty is the basis for trusting yourself, for others trusting in you, and for you trusting others. Being honest is not always easy and most times is the harder route to take, especially since most lying is rooted in fear. In addition, when you make a commitment to honesty, you must really think about the things you say to make sure they are truthful. What makes this even more difficult is that you also need to remember your words have impact and affect those around you. Honesty requires careful thought, which becomes natural once you are in the habit.

When it comes to our children, it can be so much easier to tell them untruths that we consider insignificant. I think we all catch ourselves doing it. Maybe because it is easier, maybe because we want to protect them, maybe because we don't know the answer, maybe because that is just what we do instinctively. For example, your child doesn't want to nap because he wants to stay up with all his friends. You tell him that everyone is going to nap now even though his friends are older and will not be napping. This little white lie seems so simple and harmless. But what if he finds out the truth and knows that you lied to him? Wouldn't that give him a reason to doubt your honesty the next time? And if this happened repeatedly, he then would have an even harder time believing in anything you were to say. If we set up a pattern where our children lose trust in us over the little things, we can't expect them to trust us when it comes to the bigger issues.

We need to carefully consider what we are doing when we tell our children lies, even those little white lies we think don't matter. We are setting up a pattern of behavior in which we lie to our children. The more you do anything, the easier it becomes. We are giving false information to our children who are relying on us and in a sense, distorting their reality. We are also setting up the inevitable moment when our children begin to lose trust in us.

Now we all know that we have certain little lies that are essential to our children being children, for example, Santa Claus. Santa Claus is definitely a part of the magic of being a child. My girlfriend describes the idea of Santa as "creativity." A creation that helps children believe in possibilities. Part of being a child is the wonder at what could be, the potential in life. This is what encourages children to dream. I think what we need to remember here is the intention behind what we are saying. With Santa Claus, we are encouraging our children to believe in the unimaginable. Carefully considering our intention and being conscious of what we are saying and why, is essential and helps cultivate honesty.

Other than those "essential" lies like Santa Claus, I believe there is a way to be honest in every situation that takes into consideration other necessary elements. We all know that there are adult matters that children should not have to deal with at their age. In these cases, we need to respond in a way that is truthful, yet shields them from the details that are inappropriate for them.

There are also those times when telling the truth would

be harmful to our children. In these moments, we can still be honest by stating to them that we are sorry but we are unable to share that information with them. When I do this, my child always asks why and I explain to him that there are certain things that he, as a child, does not need to know yet and that it is my job as his mom to protect him from that information. I let him know that I respect and want to be honest with him, but that he just isn't ready to comprehend what I would say. I also promise to provide him with the information as soon as the appropriate time comes. This can sound unfair, and even as I write it I can remember how unfair it would feel to me when my parents wouldn't give me answers because I was "just a child." I think the key here is our sincerity and authenticity. When our children learn to trust that we give them honest answers whenever possible and they can see that we make a true effort to do so, they are then more readily able to accept the moments when we just simply cannot. This is trust, and it is everything.

SELF-CONFIDENCE IS ESSENTIAL
Having faith in yourself is the only way your children can have faith in you.

We all know those moments when we have no clue what we are doing. Or maybe we have to make a decision or parenting choice and we aren't quite sure how to proceed. We feel nervous, and maybe even downright scared. We then lose self-confidence and sometimes second-guess our choices and actions. We lose the ability to present ourselves with authority and may even find that we are giving directions or instructions to our children in the form of a question. We may appear flustered, overwhelmed, or impatient.

Our kids have a very keen ability to notice this insecurity and can see that we are unsure. They observe this and they then become unsure of us as well. Our children rely on us to feel safe. They trust that we can take care of them, protect them, and guide them. If you don't have confidence in yourself, how are your children supposed to have confidence in you? How can they trust in your ability to keep them safe and do what is best for them?

My son provides a great example of just how much our children trust us as parents. When he gets in the shower, I test the water for him. I tell him when it's the right temperature and he walks right into the shower without checking it himself. This simple task shows how the process of trust works. I check the water temperature for my son, and it is not until I am sure that the temperature is correct that I direct him into the shower. My child trusts me and senses my confidence. He then walks into the shower relaxed and assured that he is safe with me.

This even comes into play with our newborns. New moms need to do so many things with their babies that can be foreign and scary. For example, cutting baby's fingernails, something I was scared to do the first time with my son. I spent time working through the fear prior to the task, and when I went to cut his nails, I did it with confidence and faith in my ability. My son was then able to relax and feel safe with me. Had I tried to cut his nails with self-doubt and fear surrounding me, he would have felt my anxiety and probably become nervous and agitated himself. The process would have been stressful for both of us and possibly become a negative experience.

No matter how we choose to parent and what decisions and choices we make, it's best to do so with confidence and faith. Once you make the decision to do something, do it wholeheartedly. Find ways to take away the self-doubt, second-guesses and "what-if's." If you are truly unsure, then be honest about it and share that you are not completely certain, but have made a decision that you are going to stand behind. We will all make wrong decisions. We will all make mistakes. That's OK. As we discussed earlier, making mistakes is part of parenting. It is how we grow and learn, and it is essential for our children to see that we are human.

ASK FOR HELP WHEN YOU NEED IT

The ability to ask for help is a sign of strength and confidence in your ability to parent.

If you are anything like me, asking for help is one of the hardest things to do in the world. Somehow, I learned that needing support means I'm not good enough, and can't handle whatever it is in front of me. Receiving help might also involve relinquishing control over how things are done, which is not easy at all. When it comes to our kids, asking for help is even harder because we don't want anyone to think we can't handle our own children. We've all heard the jokes about scoring points in the mommy game or being accepted into the mommy club. So, by asking for help, we may assume that we will be judged and made to feel not as capable as the rest of the moms who have it all "under control," whatever that means.

In actuality, being willing to ask for assistance and admit that things aren't "perfect" makes us better moms. Our willingness to be honest and open about our inability to do it all, all the time, shows strength of character and confidence in parenting. We've all experienced times when we attempt to do everything ourselves, and when we do, sometimes things tend to spin even more out of control. We find ourselves overwhelmed, impatient, distracted, unfocused, and anxious, to name just a few. When this happens, nobody benefits, especially our child.

When we are willing to get help in these situations, everyone is much happier. We are less frustrated and so are our kids. Nobody likes to have someone else's anxiety put on him.

Now we can even take this concept a step further and do the unimaginable, ask our children for help. From a very early age, our children are capable of lending a hand. They can carry things, hold doors, and help us find items. Asking our children for help allows them to see that we value them. Most children feel excited and proud when given the chance to help.

When we ask for help, we model for our children that asking for assistance is acceptable. That it isn't necessary to know everything or be able to do it all alone. It is so important for kids to be able to ask for help when they need it. If they need support and don't ask for it, the alternatives could be anger or frustration, not to mention giving up, acting out, and so on. We can't expect our children to be comfortable admitting they are unable to do something if we are unwilling to do the same.

You might let your child know when you are overwhelmed and need his or her help with anything from making dinner to cleaning up afterward. As your child observes you asking for support, he or she will learn to do so, too, with their own problems at school, relationships with peers, and more. We want our children to grow accustomed to asking for help when they feel lost, confused, or stressed.

GIVE EXPLANATIONS
We all deserve to know why.

As I've mentioned, I grew up with parents who felt they did not have to explain themselves to me. Any time I would ask for a reason, if my parents didn't feel like providing one, they wouldn't. I would hear, "I'm your mother and I do not have to give you a reason" or the always popular "Because I said so." I remember how unfair and frustrating these responses felt.

Everyone, including our children, deserves explanations. Whether it is to clarify why you expect certain behavior or are saying no to something your child wants. I try to explain everything; my feelings, rules, consequences and rewards. I want to give my son the opportunity to understand the decisions I make for him. Wouldn't we want explanations if somebody made decisions that affected our lives? We should be just as willing to explain to our child why he can't do something as we are willing to explain why the sky is blue. It is not that we need our children's approval, rather, we need to explain ourselves because we love and respect them.

I notice with my son that when I ask him to do something without an explanation, he is more likely to act out or display some sort of resistance. A flat out "no" invokes the desire to rebel or fight for whatever he wants to do or not do. When I give reasons, this acting out or rebelling tends to diminish or not occur at all. My son has learned to trust in my reasons due to my willingness to provide them. He understands that when I say no, I will offer an explanation that he can understand. He can trust that I have put some thought into my decision and not made a blind statement. He might not be happy about it or agree, but I give him the opportunity to understand.

When we explain to our children why, we allow them to understand more fully, observe the reasoning process, feel valued and respected, and possibly provide feedback that we might not have considered.

I think that sometimes parents might find this feedback from children somewhat threatening. Telling our children why gives them the opportunity to show us that we may have been wrong. As I mention throughout this book, we must be open to this idea of making mistakes. I find it so fascinating that my son reasons possibilities as to why a decision I make might be incorrect. Often we have full conversations where we go back and forth dissecting a problem. Sometimes in the end my decision stands, but other times he has shown me a different perspective and my decision changes. Either way, the opportunity this provides for conversation, and for my son to feel he is an active decision maker in his life, is priceless.

SOMETIMES IT ACTUALLY IS ALL ABOUT YOU

Taking an honest look at yourself can provide a deeper understanding of the behaviors of those around you.

Whenever I've noticed my son is acting out or if he and I are going through a period of disconnection, the first thing I consider is whether he is undergoing some sort of transition. Is he about to start walking or talking? Is he attending a new school, or trying a new sport? When big milestones like this are about to happen, I have noticed that there may be some miscommunication between parent and child. I believe that the child has all his attention focused on the big task in front of him. Sometimes children can become increasingly self-centered as they are about to attempt something new that requires their complete attention.

If I have ruled out any sort of major transition, then I immediately look at myself. Is there anything my child is trying to tell me or make me aware of that I am not noticing? Is there something I could possibly be avoiding because I don't want to deal with it? Whatever the reason may be, I check in with myself to see how my own "stuff" might be influencing or affecting my son's behavior.

We are usually so quick to notice when our children are misbehaving or driving us crazy. It is also important for us to realize just how big of an effect we have on our children. Our kids are so attuned to us that when we have things going on internally, they react to our pain, sadness, and so on. They also want us to understand them and their needs. When we are unresponsive or distracted, they will try to make us see. This is how I think of acting out, it's a way for our children to reflect back to us what we are feeling inside. It's also a way for our children to show us what they are feeling without using words.

I remember my son and I spending one week almost completely disconnected from each other. I noticed that he was acting differently than his normal easygoing and happy self. He was irritable, frustrated, and misbehaving. Then, I began to notice my own behavior. I was very easily frustrated myself, impatient, and foggy-headed.

As I realized this, I assessed what might be going on with me. What should have been so obvious was not, but I was finally seeing it. My best friend and I were in the midst of an argument and not speaking. I thought I was keeping my feelings under control, but I figured out through my son's behavior, that I was not. I needed to resolve my inner conflict so that my son could have his mother back.

Examples like this are there for each of us. We all try to put aside things that we need to deal with at times. How amazing is it that if we simply look and listen to our children they can mirror to us the truth of what we are feeling. What an absolute gift if we allow it.

BE YOUR CHILD'S OWN PERSONAL CHEERLEADER

Imagine being encouraged every step of the way through your life journey.

My girlfriend and I were hanging out one day and she was feeling down. I decided to be silly and performed a cheer to lift her spirits. Although it was funny, the cheer ended up making a big difference for her. We then discussed what life would be like if we had our own cheerleader following us around and rooting us on to success. As we spoke, it hit me that this is exactly what I do as a mother. It also occurred to me that this is probably one of the most essential functions as a parent, whether we realize it or not. If we become conscious of this role, how much more effective it can be in our children's lives.

It is important to note here that what I am discussing is very different from over praising and making our children believe that they are better or more special than those around them, which can be harmful. The praise I am speaking of is grounded in truth and sincerity and is simply a supportive gesture to let our children know that they can trust that we are always by their sides.

As our children move through life, it is our job to support them as they maneuver through obstacles. I can remember a clear example of my son learning how to go up the stairs by himself. I would stand behind him the whole way, cheer him on, and tell him what a good job he was doing. As he learned how to eat by himself, I would praise his progress. I can remember the look on my son's face and the sheer joy he must have felt at me not only watching him, but cheering for him. I could tell that he wanted to keep going simply because he had the attention and appreciation of a loving audience.

I do think that as our children get older, being their personal cheerleader can become more challenging. Especially when our children might be learning and attempting things that are unfamiliar to us, or don't meet our approval. In addition, our children tend to push us away as they get older to gain their own independence. This is natural and necessary. What is important is to continue to be by their sides, cheering them on and rooting for them. Although they might appear to find your "cheering" annoying, inside I think they secretly know and appreciate the fact that their parents are encouraging them and supporting them even in the face of challenge and opposition.

MIND YOUR MANNERS
Your children learn by example.

We all tell our children how important it is to have manners. We want our kids to be polite when they are outside the home and in the world. We want them to represent the family well and put us in a good light.

I am not sure that we all realize how important it is for us to mind our own manners as well. It is essential that we lead and inspire our children through example. Children are better able to learn things that they observe, rather than what they hear. Therefore, it is so imperative that we use our manners with one another, and our children.

For example, saying please and thank you to our children is something we can sometimes overlook. When we ask them to do things around the house or when they do their chores, I think that we might take for granted that we should acknowledge these behaviors with gratitude. Even if your child is doing something that is expected of him, a please and thank you can go a long way toward helping a child to feel respected and appreciated as part of the family system.

 When children feel respected by others and observe respect in action, they will be more likely to act in kind as they make their ways through the world. Respect is essential to our children succeeding in life, and is the foundation for healthy friendships, mature love, and successful work partnerships.

Our children will also learn self-respect from us. As we model our manners, they will see themselves as worthy of respect. This self-respect carries over to the choices our children will make throughout their lives. It will form the basis for the type of friends they associate with, the personal choices they make regarding drug and alcohol use, and the way they allow others to treat them. If a child has high self-appreciation, he will command the same from those around him, and will not allow others to mistreat or disregard them.

By always using our manners, we develop a habit of

respect. We cannot expect our children to show us courtesy if we are not providing the same to them. There are so many ways to practice this throughout the day. For example, we can say thank you to our child after leaving a store where he behaved well. Or, we can ask our child to please clean his room. These are simple examples, yet an acknowledgement blanketed in appreciation can mean more to our children than we can even imagine.

PATIENCE IS MORE THEN A VIRTUE

Patience provides an opening within you to allow the present to unfold fully without interference.

One of my biggest concerns before having my son was my lack of patience. I would find myself easily frustrated with others doing things more slowly than I would. I believed I had to do things myself to get them done quickly, efficiently, and correctly. I worried that I would somehow use this attitude with my child and knew very well that this would not be healthy for him or me.

In my opinion, having patience is probably one of the biggest parenting challenges. There are so many things happening at once and so much that needs to be done. Then, we have these little human beings with us and we realize very quickly that they move more slowly and take their time. Suddenly our ability to be quick and efficient is challenged, and it's hard to find a way to embrace that slower pace.

As I mentioned earlier, I have learned that the ability to be able to "sit and do nothing" is a valuable skill. Being quiet with our inner selves without any distraction can be difficult but worthwhile. We can practice remaining present in the moment by simply sitting and breathing. At first, we might feel unsettled, but eventually those feelings of discontent dissipate. After practicing this and making it a habit, settling into silence becomes a much more attainable process. Once we are able to do this, we will then find it helpful when we need to find patience with our children. We will find we are able to breathe through the agitation and discontent we may feel throughout the day and remain present and at our child's level.

Our ability to remain patient is a skill that is essential for our children's development. As we all know, as our children grow older they seek independence and the ability to do things for themselves. What I have found is that if you can find a way to allow your child to take his time to do what he needs to do, many positive things result. First, children are able to feel a sense of accomplishment and capability that is so essential to their growth. Second, the task at hand is completed quicker than had the typical "we're in a rush just let me do it" argument ensued. Third, both mom and child are much happier.

Many of us are on tight schedules. I certainly rush around in the morning with a million things to do and what feels like not enough time. However, finding a way to stay patient and calm actually adds time to your day. We are able to accomplish more when we are relaxed because we think more clearly.

YOU ARE NOW A STUDENT FOR LIFE

Be open to the idea that your children are your teachers. You will learn more about yourself through your relationship with them than from any other relationship in your life.

learn from my son every single day. He is the best teacher I've ever had in my life. Yet, so many of us are caught up in our jobs as teachers to our children. There is so much we have to show them, so many lessons for them to learn. We spend our days disciplining, answering questions, providing care, and so on and so on. It is part of our job as parents to teach our children, a very important part, but we can also be students.

Our children provide us with insight into who we are as human beings. Through them, we discover so much about ourselves, like how we handle setbacks, how we deal with frustration, how we process fear, and so on. We perceive the world differently by viewing it through our children's eyes, and on a smaller scale, can even learn how to build train tracks or use our i-Phone apps. If we pay attention and stay open, we can gain knowledge and insight through our kids.

Better yet, our children can inspire us to learn, grow, and find ways to live from the highest part of ourselves. For example, my son has a beautiful way of honoring his own needs. He remains compassionate to how other people might feel, while still standing up for himself. Watching him has motivated me to do the same. Instead of ignoring my own needs so I don't hurt another person, I have learned through my son to honor myself, set boundaries, and be kind to others in the process.

In addition, as our children teach and inspire us, we need to be willing to openly acknowledge our "student status" to them. Children take great pride in teaching, especially their parents. Simply saying "thank you, I didn't know that" can validate your children's help. Knowing that they have successfully shared knowledge with an adult that they love is a tremendous boost to their confidence and sense of self worth. I love the smile on my son's face and the glint of wonder in his eyes when I let him know that he has taught me something new. It is priceless.

DISCIPLINE WITH POSITIVE PURPOSE

How beautiful and peaceful our world would be if
everyone acted in love and kindness.
You can seize the opportunity to make
your family home that beautiful and peaceful place.

We can often find ourselves at the end of our rope when we are disciplining our children. When we let emotion take over, our ability to think rationally and remember our intentions and reasons for discipline becomes challenging. It is in these times that we might tend to overreact and lose sight of the situation at hand. When I discipline my son, I strive to do it with kindness and love. It is important to remember to not take others' behavior personally, including the behavior of our children. Believe me, I know how challenging this can be on a daily basis. However, if we choose kindness as part of our intention, then I truly do believe it will significantly alter how we discipline for the better.

Furthermore, we need to understand why we are disciplining and explain those reasons to our children. Rules are intended to protect our children, not to control or inhibit them. They can provide a safety net that allows children the freedom to be who they are and explore the world as they see necessary. Remember, these are their journeys and lives. We are simply granted the gift of being their parent and an important person in their world. When we keep this purpose in mind, it becomes much easier to stay in a place of love and kindness when we are setting rules or following through with consequences.

I trust that when we discipline our children in this way they are more receptive to what we say and are better able to understand our motivation. As stated earlier, I think that explaining everything to our children is so essential, and this extends to discipline. They may not agree with our choices as parents, but they can respect them because they understand our intentions.

In addition, this goes back to creating good habits. The more we practice stopping, breathing, and remaining present, the more easily we will be able to initiate these behaviors when we need to discipline. Being able to take a step back and think gives us a chance to remember why we are disciplining in the first place and deliver the consequences in a loving and caring manner.

PARENTING IS A CHALLENGE AND A JOY... YOU CAN DO IT

It is not your job to please and spoil your children, rather to guide them toward becoming capable human beings in the world.

Sometimes being a parent is just plain hard. We have to do things that don't feel comfortable and that we wish we didn't have to do. The worst part comes when we have to hurt our child's feelings or "break their hearts." Even worse, is when your children come to that point when they say they officially hate you. Nobody wants their children to be mad at them. Nobody wants to break his or her child's heart. However, sometimes it is our job as parents to make those hard decisions because it is our responsibility to keep our children safe and give them the tools they need to succeed as adults.

I've observed so many moms give in to their children from day one. I've heard so many empty threats and broken promises. For example, how many times have you told your child, "If I count to three...," or "If you do that one more time..." Parents use these statements daily. Saying them is the easy part, but following through is another story.

It is so important to realize that once the statement is made, the follow through is the most essential component. Our children are looking to us to see if we will do what we say. They might kick and scream, but in all honesty, they not only require consequences, they crave them because it brings order to their world.

Discipline shows our children that we have a sense of what we are doing and know our boundaries and the boundaries we are setting for them. In a sense, rules are the way we tell our children that they can make mistakes within a certain safe limit. We have a clear understanding of the boundaries and are not scared to enforce them to keep our children safe. Rules provide children with a sense of freedom to take risks knowing that their parents "have their backs."

Our children are testing us to see how much they can trust

us. They want to know just how far they can go before we are unwilling or unable to step up to the plate and do whatever it takes, no matter how difficult it may be. I believe this is as true when our children are two as when they are sixteen. Our kids outwardly do not like the rules, but on the inside they are able to rest easy because they know they are cared for and safe. If we are unable to stand up for our children when they are young and make the hard decisions, then we will certainly not be able to do it when they are older.

I use time outs with my son only when necessary. They occur infrequently, but every time out is met with great resistance. It once took me two hours of sitting on the floor with my toddler son for him to complete a 30-second time out. The important lesson for both of us was that I was not going to give in, no matter what. His resistance effort has not been as drastic since then, but he usually does not go willingly. My rule is that he must settle down and sit quietly for his time out period. Fidgeting, crying, and yelling are not allowed. The time out begins when he is sitting still and will start over if at any time during the time out he begins to protest. After his time out is completed, I ask him to tell me why he was in time out and to apologize. I then give him giant hug and kiss and tell him how much I love him.

The interesting thing is that after each time out, there is a clear difference in my son's attitude before and after the time out. Afterward, he is extremely loving and affectionate and tells me how much he loves me, usually numerous times. I almost get the sense that he is thanking me for the time out and for helping him refocus.

BE WILLING TO BE VULNERABLE
It is only through vulnerability that true
strength can arise.

When we become parents, I believe that we are more emotionally vulnerable than at any other time in our lives. This is because the deep and indescribable love we feel for our children automatically makes us realize the pain we would experience should something bad happen to them. So many possibilities for hurt exist in this world and the thought of our loved one harmed in any way breaks our hearts, leaving us vulnerable.

Often times, vulnerability is perceived as a weakness and for many it can be frightening. It can be very uncomfortable to feel so suddenly raw and exposed. When we get scared, we often have a tendency to put up a guard and use our defenses to push away whatever is causing our fear. We often times use our defenses to ease the discomfort and fear that we are feeling as the result of becoming a parent, instead of embracing our vulnerability and using it to be better parents.

The tendency might be to act as if we are invincible, that we can handle anything and nothing can harm us. I do believe that we can manage what comes our way, but I also know that we will suffer pain throughout life. That pain is where all the lessons and growth lie. Being willing to embrace the pain as it comes, rather than seek to avoid it is how we can use our vulnerability as a tool.

Embracing vulnerability as a parent allows us to keep our hearts open and remain in a loving space with our children, a space that fosters mutual respect and understanding. Taking a risk without knowing the outcome, asking for help or saying I don't know, are all ways in which we are vulnerable. When we are able to do these things with our children, we not only open pathways for deeper connection, we also teach our children that being vulnerable is not something to be feared. In experiencing our vulnerability, they develop a comfort with their own.

DON'T TAKE YOURSELF TOO SERIOUSLY

Smile, laugh, and find humor in this very important job of parenting.

During our jobs as parents, we must be able to look in the mirror at the end of the day and not be hard on ourselves. We all make mistakes and will continue to do so, and often. If we can find the lightness and humor in it all, then we will be able to remember that parenting is actually supposed to be enjoyable.

When people ask me how I like being a mother, my first reaction is always to say it's fun. I hear many people talk about parenting as challenging, stressful, and exhausting, but I rarely hear moms talk about the fun. I believe that being a mother is the most fun I've had in my life. There is not a single day that goes by where I don't have a full belly laugh, roll around on the floor, and sing silly songs.

I am certainly not saying that I don't have my difficult moments of stress and exhaustion, because I do. But as I've written in previous chapters, I do set the intention at the beginning of my day to enjoy my child and my role as his mother. With this intention set, I can find my way more easily out of frustration and fatigue. If you tune into your child for even five minutes, I guarantee he will do something to make you laugh or smile. It's instant happiness.

It is through our children that we truly get to be children ourselves again. By not taking ourselves too seriously, we can let go of some stress, and have a good time with parenting. Funny thing is, once we start making it fun, parenting doesn't seem nearly as stressful or exhausting. If you think about it, when things are fun they automatically become easier. We have this amazing opportunity to show our children the happiness we feel by being their parents and the joy we experience by seeing the world through their eyes.

ALL YOU NEED IS LOVE
Practice love in thought and action.

Ultimately, the most important thing we have to give our children is our love -- our full, unconditional, and unwavering love. Children should never have to question our feelings. Without a doubt, they should always know their parents love them. My son and I have a little game where we say that we love each other "even though." I love you even though you hurt my feelings. I love you even though you had a hard time listening. I love you even though your choice was an unfair one. I let him know that no matter what may happen, nothing will ever change my love for him and that is something he can count on forever.

It is important that our children learn to take this concept of "loving even though" with them throughout their lives. There will be times when they are wronged, suffer a broken heart, or experience cruelty. Throughout all adversity, we need to teach our children to love. I read a quote not too long ago that was written by a six-year-old child, which said "Show me someone you hate and I will show you what love really is." We as parents need to be the source of filling our children with love so they can bring that love into the world. My goal is to raise a child not only capable of showing love, but also willing to live it in the face of darkness.

It is essential to show love to our children as well as tell them we love them. Giving hugs and kisses, and sharing laughter, are all ways that we can demonstrate our feelings to our children. Most of all, we need to be able to say I love you. To look our children in the eyes and tell them how we feel. My son and I say I love you to one another probably 10 times a day. Whenever I feel it, whenever the thought even crosses my mind, I make it a point to say it aloud, and he does the same. How great it feels when your child is engrossed in a game of trains and he stops to yell, "Mommy, I love you!" from across the room.

Our children need to know that they can make mistakes and take risks without having to worry about losing our love. At times, they will disappoint us and make us angry, but they should never lose our love. It is up to us to communicate this to them clearly and teach them how to "love even though."

LETTER TO MY READERS: I'M NOT AN EXPERT, JUST A MOM WHO LOVES HER SON

I began writing this book as a gift to my son. I thought it would be a loving insight into why I chose to parent him as I did. As the book started coming together, I decided I wanted to share these concepts with anyone who would be willing to read them. If you are reading this now, then I am happy to say, my intention was served.

When I began this book, my son's father and I were married, and as I mentioned at the beginning of the book, have decided to divorce. I feel this is an important issue to address along with what I have written. My ex-husband and I were together for sixteen years, and eventually found that we were no longer happy by one another's side. Without this happiness, I believe there was no way that my son could be happy either.

I don't believe that my son has suffered as a result of his father and I divorcing, rather I think he has prospered. I hear so many people say that they choose to stay together because of the kids, even though they are unhappy. I believe that this is actually a worse situation for our children. Our children know when we are unhappy and untrue to ourselves. It not only hurts them, but also teaches them a distorted image of love and happiness.

I do acknowledge that my son has suffered a great loss, but I also believe that strength and character are born through our difficulties. As a result of my decision to change our family system, my son has received the chance to see who I am. He has watched me survive the hardest thing I have ever had to do in my life. He has watched me come to know the person I am inside and find the courage to live true to myself. He has had the chance to witness true happiness and authenticity. He finally has his mother. I am proud of the decision I made and where I stand today.

I tell my son that all families look different. We come in all different varieties, but the most important thing is that we love each other. I cherish being a mother and have had the best five years experiencing all it has to offer me. I look forward to all the challenges that lie ahead and believe that the concepts I have written here have provided a strong foundation.

Whether you agree or disagree with what you have read, I hope this book has made you think. I hope that you have been inspired to try something different. Most of all, I hope that you are a little bit more willing to open your heart and be vulnerable with those beautiful beings surrounding you.

That said, my son is now just five. If you really want to see if my parenting philosophies served me well, check back in 13 years...

ABOUT THE AUTHOR

Jennifer Laurent was born and raised in Rockland County, New York. She has a BA in Psychology, a Masters Degree in Clinical Social Work, a teaching certification in yoga, and is a certified NLP life coach and hypnotherapist. Jennifer has worked as a rape crisis counselor and drug and alcohol counselor. She has provided therapy to struggling families and dying and disabled children and their families. She has also worked in Emergency Room/Trauma social work. Jennifer Laurent writes for *LiveThroughTheHeart.com* and resides in Southern California with her son. *Excerpts from the Heart of a Mom* is her first book and she is currently working on a second.

www.livethroughtheheart.com

Visit and subscribe to read more about conscious living by Jennifer Laurent.

The following pages contain examples of what you will find.

MOTHERHOOD

For me, being a mother is a beautiful truth that is beyond words. That indescribable feeling that is difficult to explain yet is one of the most real and profound experiences of my life. It brings me joy and fulfillment each and every day and has caused my heart to burst open wider than I ever dreamed possible. It is because of my son that I am capable of loving and forgiving in the way that I do. It is because of him that I am the person I am today, and for that and so much more, I am filled with gratitude.

My journey through motherhood has taught me more about myself than any other life experience I have lived. Each and every day I eagerly embrace my role as student, willing to open my mind and expand my heart to whatever is to come my way. I have been challenged to face fears and achieve goals. I have been inspired to look honestly within myself in an effort to live my truth. I have been excited to experience the uncertainty that parenting promises with curiosity and an open heart.

When I think about being a mother I become full of an overwhelming sense of unconditional love and joy. This intense feeling is one that I truly believe has the power to transform the world. Through experiencing this sense of love for my son I have learned to love myself in a way unknown to me before. I have learned to embrace and accept all of who I am in the same way I am able to embrace and accept my child. This gift of self- love has been a powerful one and has truly transformed my entire existence.

To be completely honest, finding the words to write this has been a struggle for me. Motherhood has always been something that I simply felt I was meant to do. It is something I feel in my heart, allowing my sense of truth to guide me. It has taken my journey throughout this universe to great heights and it will continue to expand my world far and wide. I will continue to learn, grow, and be challenged. Most of all I will continue to love with a far greater capacity than I can even imagine right now. That's the magic of being a mother; over and over, just when you think you can't possibly love any more than you already do your heart expands and connects you to even deeper parts of your soul and greater heights of love.

A HEARTFELT APOLOGY

I know we all have rough days, weeks, years even? Well it has definitely been a rough two weeks for me. In dealing with some inner conflict and disappointment I had a very difficult time maintaining my patience and ability to focus. Totally understandable, yet it is my four-year old son who had to be on the receiving side. This is certainly not a fun or fair position for him to have to be in.

I know that when I am emotionally distracted my patience level goes down and my frustration level goes up. I tend to be short tempered and can even yell. I lose my sense of humor and lightheartedness. I am simply just not the same mom that I usually am. I am not saying that I am ever perfect, but I am usually a very focused and present parent that has fun with my son and truly has a ton of patience. As I start to lose myself I am very aware of it, yet can't seem to take control. It is frustrating for me and for my little family as a whole.

As I worked my way through the last couple of weeks I made sure to be very open with my little guy. I let him know that I was struggling, continuously apologized to him, and told him how much I love him. I know that these behaviors were certainly helpful, but they were in no way a substitute for the mom my son is accustomed to.

Upon finally coming out of my inner turmoil I sat down with my son and discussed the prior weeks with him. I let him know that I felt that I was past the difficulties I had been struggling with and that he could look forward to having his mom back. I apologized again and let him know that I understood how difficult the past weeks must have been for him. He responded by letting me know that it had been a struggle for him and that he was really happy that I was feeling better. He then decided to get up and come over to hug me and let me know that he loved me very much.

I was able to see very clearly in my son's eyes how important it was that I had validated his feelings and struggles by taking the time to sit with him and sincerely explain and apologize. I believe that had I not directly acknowledged it our lives would have went on as normal but deep inside him there may have been some confusion or unawareness as to what had happened and how he had been feeling. I believe that this simple five-minute conversation turned a negative mother/child situation into one of the most memorable and heartfelt experiences my son and I have shared.

I know we all have these times with our children. It is part of life that we can not always be our best. Our best is ever changing and so is the world and circumstances around us. I think that what is most important though, is how we honor ourselves and the little people we share our world with in these moments of struggle. I encourage you now to try this with your children. If you have been struggling or

think there is any reason this may be an effective conversation to have with your child please do. I look forward
to hearing all about your experiences: the conversations,
responses, results, etc. I am so excited to hear from you!